FUN CRAFTS FOR KIDS

Fun CRAFTS FOR KIDS

There is an ever-growing understanding of the importance of creative arts and crafts for young children. Parents and educators appreciate the need to provide opportunities for self-expression, the use of imagination and achievements that reflect the growth of important physical skills. Children of every age benefit from the activities which develop awareness through observation, touch, smell and hearing.

These pages are for everyone who spends time with, and cares for, young children. The activities in this book are intended only as a guide. Be sensitive to your children's own ideas and adapt these methods to them and to your available resources. And ***please*** *don't let children copy directly from the book . . . encourage them to experiment, and "do their own thing"!*

The activities described here can be done by most four year olds. You will often need to simplify tasks for a two year old, though a three year old may be able to manage them with little or no help. Encourage older children to use the activities as a starting point for extending their own levels of skill. With most activities we have included a section called ***Other things to try*** *which often includes ideas for older children, as well as adding variety to simple activities for the younger child.*

The crafts are grouped according to technique rather than skill level, but where possible the most simple one comes first in each group. Each activity begins with HAVE READY *which lists necessary materials, followed by* GET SET *which lists the steps for preparation and finally comes the fun part,* GO!

Steps marked * should be performed by an adult or at least under adult supervision, depending on your child and the particular situation.

One secret for successful creative play is "be prepared." Work in a place where mess doesn't matter and where unfinished work can be left to be completed later. Have on hand a box of old clothes to use as smocks, plastic sheeting to protect the work area and any other bits and pieces you think might come in handy for crafting, like cardboard rolls, bits of foil and fabric, lengths of colored yarn and so on. Your throwaways can be a young child's art material and treasure.

Perhaps the most important ingredient in the process is FUN! This book is all about having fun in a creative way and sharing these good experiences with your child.

CONTENTS

Managing Editor: Judy Poulos
Editorial Coordinator: Margaret Kelly
Design and Production: Amanda Westwood; Nadia Sbisa; Margie Mulray; Chris Hatcher
Cover Design: Frank Pithers
Photography: Andrew Elton
Publisher: Philippa Sandall

ISBN 0 937769 26 6

PAINTING

Painting opens up a child's world of color and imagination. Children love the experience of brushing, spattering, dripping, squeezing and squelching paint on paper. The resulting picture is much less important than the creative process and the enjoyment of the experience.

The first stage of painting lies in the joy of experimenting with color. You have only to provide the equipment, opportunity and encouragement, then stand back and let it all happen!

Painting is bound to make quite a mess — so be prepared. Find a spot where splatters don't matter or "carpet" the area with layers of newspaper. A painting smock is a good idea but one of Dad's old shirts will do just as well. Have a bucket or bowl of soapy water and a sponge on hand for cleaning up drips and splashes.

Very young children prefer to paint sitting down on the floor or standing at a low table. An older child often feels more comfortable with an easel. Of course you don't have to rush out and buy an easel — simply find a place where you can tape, peg or pin (with some child-proof push pins) some paper at the appropriate height. Find a suitable spot for the painting to hang or lay flat until dry.

What you need

Brushes Brushes with long, fairly thick handles are easiest for children to control. Start with thick brushes 1 – 1½ inches (200-250 mm) wide and add finer brushes later on. If possible, have one brush for each color of paint or provide clean water and a rag for cleaning brushes between colors. Teach your child how to clean the brushes after painting and to store them, bristles up, in a jar or bottle.

Paints Whether you choose powdered or pre-mixed paints, make sure that they are clearly marked *non-toxic*. Water-based paints, such as tempera and watercolors are best for children. They usually clean up easily with soap and water. Start with the basic colors of red, yellow and blue with black and white. Mixing these will provide a variety of colors and, with the addition of white or black, you can also vary the shade. Don't forget to mix black and white to make gray.

Paper Children prefer to work on fairly large sheets of paper. A pad of newsprint paper, available at art supply stores, is perfect for the job. Paper of different colors and sizes can spark a child's imagination. Try colored construction paper, poster board, brown craft paper or grocery bags. The back sides of computer printouts are also good for painting and drawing.

Containers Any old jar, cup or plastic container is fine for holding paint. The container should be clean and should not topple over when a brush is left standing in it. Remember not to overfill the container: 1-1½ inches (2-3 cm) of paint is enough. An aluminum muffin pan makes a great mixing tray.

Items for experiments Different types of paints and dyes, as well as different painting tools, can fuel a child's creativity. Liquid food coloring (available at supermarkets) and edible vegetable dyes (available at art supply stores) can be brushed on like watercolor paint. Cellulose sponges and crumpled aluminum foil can be used to dab paint in interesting patterns. Paint rollers and different types of brushes (toothbrushes, for example) are also good painting tools. In this chapter, we've also encouraged painting with feathers, drinking straws, cotton balls, rope and plastic spoons.

Covers and protectors Before anyone starts painting be sure to protect clothing and work surfaces with washable or disposable covers and protectors. Cover surfaces with newspapers, plastic sheets (including old shower curtains or raincoats) or old bed sheets. The cheapest and most accessible covering for tables and floor is, of course, plain old newspaper. Remember that a disposable cover is preferable to one that requires washing. Use one of Mom or Dad's old shirts, a wipeable bib apron or old plastic raincoat as a painting smock. In a pinch, a large plastic trash bag does the trick. Cut out openings for the child's head and arms and slip the bag over his head.
Note: *Never let a child have access to large plastic bags without an adult's supervision.*

Painting on paper

● HAVE READY
paint and brushes
large sheet of paper
masking tape (optional)
● GET SET
Protect floor area.
Position containers of paint and brushes in a safe position close to paper.
Secure paper in position with masking tape (if necessary).
● GO
When finished, hang painting somewhere safe to dry.

Easel painting

● HAVE READY
paint and brushes
large sheet of paper
easel, board or suitable wall surface
push pins, bulldog or spring clips, clothespins or tape
● GET SET
Protect floor area.
Position paint and brushes in convenient place, close to easel.
Secure paper to easel with pins, clips or tape.
● GO
When finished, hang painting somewhere safe to dry.

Object painting

● HAVE READY
paint
brushes
large sheet of paper
easel or board
clothespins, clips or tape
objects such as sticks, feathers, rope, sponge, cotton balls, shaving brushes, bunches of dried grass and so on

● GET SET
Set up as for *Easel painting*.

● GO
Dip various objects in paint and brush or dab them on paper.

Other things to try

- ***Provide several shades of only one color, plus black and white.***
- ***Let colors set a theme such as sunny, cold, happy or sad.***
- ***Vary the shape and size of the paper. Try different colors and textures of paper including wallpaper, wrapping paper, wax paper, paper toweling, boxes and paper bags.***
- ***Make the paint watery or add sand, detergent, salt or sugar for different effects.***
- ***For older children, try paper with patterns or holes in it.***

Water painting

● HAVE READY
bucket or bowl
broad brush
water

● GET SET
Fill bucket with water.
Tie brush to the bucket with string so it doesn't get lost.
Find a suitable surface for painting such as paths, walls, fences and so on.

● GO
"Paint" with the water on the surface.

Other things to try

- ***Use paint rollers.***
- ***"Paint" a shadow.***
- ***Add a few drops of paint to color the water.***

Blow painting

● HAVE READY
thin paint
straws, one for each child
non-absorbent paper
spoon
newspaper

● GET SET
Spread newspaper on flat surface. Place paper on top.
Using spoon, drip paint onto paper.

● GO
Blowing gently through straw, spread paint around paper to make patterns.
Dry flat.

Other things to try

- ***When paint is dry, add details to picture with felt tip pens or crayons.***

Crayon & paint

● HAVE READY
crayons in light colors
paper and newspaper
broad brushes
non-toxic, dark color paint thinned with a lot of water,
or watercolor paints

● GET SET
Make a pad with several sheets of newspaper. Place drawing paper on top.

● GO
Press down with crayons to make a thick, waxy drawing. Cover drawing with paint. Dry flat.
This is a great way to use up all the crayons that are too light for regular coloring.

Other things to try

■ ***Make a "magic drawing" by using a white candle to draw on white paper. A picture will magically appear when paint is applied.***

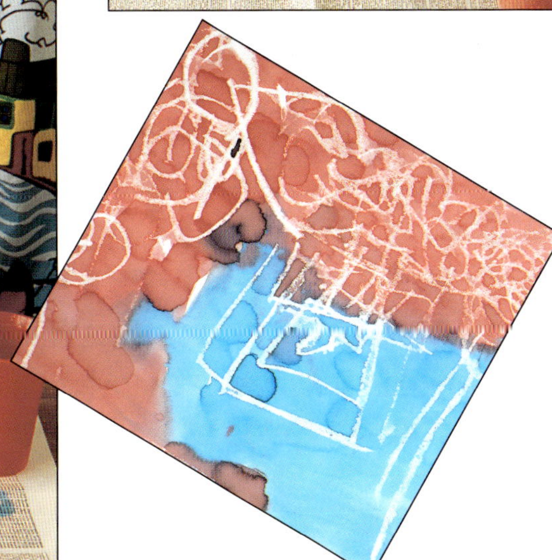

Bubble painting

● HAVE READY
powdered, non-toxic paint
dishwashing liquid
bowls or plastic containers
drinking straws
paper

● GET SET
Put some dishwashing liquid into a separate bowl for each color. Mix some paint with a small quantity of water and add the liquid paint to dishwashing liquid to make a strong color. *Note:* IT IS VERY IMPORTANT TO MAKE SURE THE CHILD KNOWS HOW TO BLOW THROUGH A STRAW BEFORE THIS NEXT STEP.

● GO
Put straw in liquid and keep blowing until bubbles rise higher than sides of bowl.
Make a print of bubbles by placing a sheet of paper gently on top of bubbles, without breaking them. Repeat this step for each color. Dry painting flat.

Other things to try

■ ***Paint a picture around the bubble print with a paintbrush and paint.***

Foil painting

● HAVE READY
foil
non-toxic acrylic or tempera paint
liquid soap
brushes

● GET SET
Cut foil to painting size.
If using tempera, add 2-3 drops of liquid soap to paint.

● GO
Paint on foil as you would on paper. This technique is especialy good for winter or holiday paintings.

Other things to try

- ***Use cellophane instead of foil.***
- ***Paint with thin brushes.***

Foil etching

● HAVE READY
foil
cardboard
tape
non-toxic tempera paint in a dark color
liquid soap
broad brush
pencil or twig

● GET SET
Mix 2-3 drops of liquid soap with tempera paint. Secure foil to cardboard with tape.

● GO
Brush on paint to cover foil. Let dry. Using stick or pencil, scratch dry paint from foil to make patterns or picture. Be careful not to tear foil.

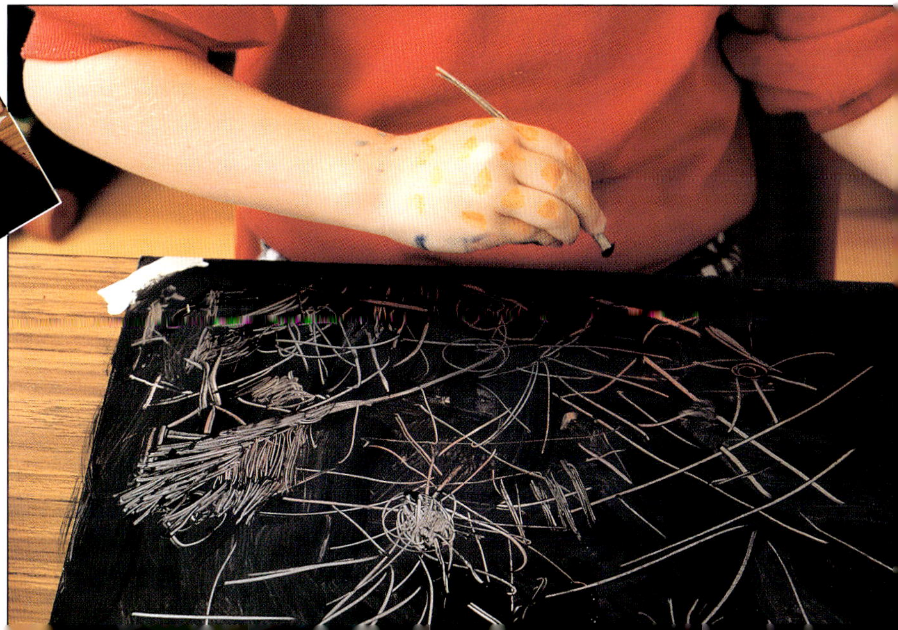

Wet paper painting

● HAVE READY
paper
water
sponge
non-toxic thin paint
small spoons
brushes

● GET SET
On a flat surface, use sponge to wet paper thoroughly.

● GO
Drip paint onto wet paper with brush or spoon. Allow colors to blend. Children may wish to go further, using a clean brush to mix colors and develop patterns.
Dry flat.

Other things to try

■ ***Paint picture on dry paper and when it is dry run it under water to blur the colors.***

Mixing colors

● HAVE READY
powdered, non-toxic paint in blue, red, yellow, black and white
spoons and aluminum muffin pan or small plastic containers
water and brushes
paper and newspaper

● GET SET Spread out newspaper on the work surface. Have paper ready for painting. Measure out small quantities of powdered paint.

● GO
Spoon a very small amount of two colors of paint powder into a container. Dip brush into water and mix powder with wet brush to make paint. Use this brush for painting. Wash brushes in clean water between mixes.

Other things to try

■ ***Use liquid vegetable dyes or food colorings instead of paint, adding color with an eye dropper.***

Blots and ...

● HAVE READY
non-toxic paint
brush, spoon or flat stick
paper
● GET SET
Fold paper in half then open it out flat. Place paper on flat surface.
● GO
With brush, spoon or stick, put drops of paint on one half of paper, beginning near fold. Fold paper again and rub palms of hands over paper, starting at fold and working out to edges. Open paper out to see the colorful blot.

Other things to try

- ***Cut out shapes to decorate a wall, hang in the breeze or fly on a mobile (see pages 16-17).***
- ***Make blots on small pieces of firm paper and use these for cards and gift tags.***

Butterflies

Make a wonderful rainbow butterfly mobile in exactly the same way as the blots on page 15 by putting the paint along the fold of the paper for the body and blotting the color where the wings should be. Paint on the feelers later. Cut out the butterflies, attach them to string and tie them to a wire hanger. Hang them up to fly in the breeze.

String painting

● HAVE READY
non-toxic paint
string or yarn
brushes
hinged clothespins
paper

● GET SET
Cut lengths of string or yarn 12-18 inches (30-50 cm) long.
Lay paper on a flat surface.

● GO
Holding one end of string with a clothespin, dip string into paint. You may need a brush to help coat string completely. Drape strings onto paper, making patterns. Lift strings off. Dry flat.

Other things to try

■ ***Fold paper as for blot painting. Lay painted string on one side of paper, leaving clothespin hanging over edge. Fold paper again and holding paper firmly with one hand, pull string out from inside paper with other hand. Open paper and repeat process with same or different colors.***

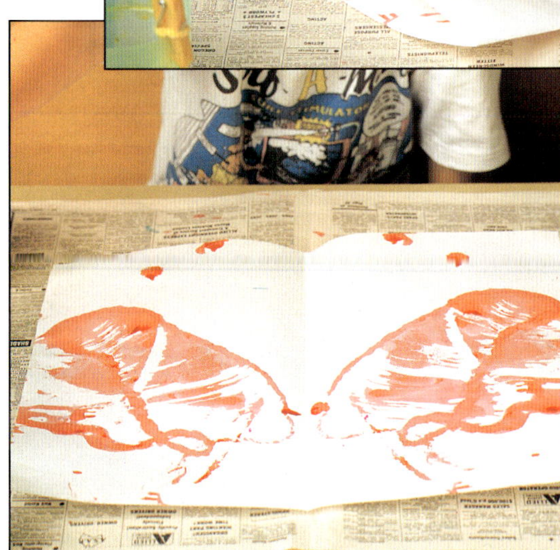

People painting

● HAVE READY
paper, large sheet or roll
non-toxic, wide felt-tip pen
non-toxic paint
brushes
scissors (optional)

● GET SET
Place child-sized sheet of paper on the ground. Draw around child, making body outline.

● GO
Paint "portrait" inside outline.
Figure can be cut out and used for play or as a wall decoration.

Other things to try

- ***Make a family of "people" including baby, adults and even a favorite teddy bear.***
- ***Decorate "people" with scraps of materials, colored paper, yarn and odds and ends of fabric for clothes, hair, eyes and so on.***

Mural people

● HAVE READY
same list of items as for *People painting (see page 19)*
tape, clothespins,clothesline, cord

● GET SET
Make individual "paper" people or tape them together.
Tie cord between two trees.

● GO
Cut holes for faces in the "people." Suspend the mural on the clothesline or cord, so that children can stand behind it with their faces peeping through.

Other things to try

■ ***Use an old white bed sheet instead of paper.***

■ ***Children can bring the mural to life, singing songs and telling stories as if each painting were a character in a story. An adult will often have to ask questions to get the action started.***

Paper chains

HAVE READY
a completed drawing or painting
ruler
pencil
scissors
paste or stapler

GET SET
Place drawing wrong side up on a flat surface and use ruler to draw lines, dividing it into strips. Cut along lines. Older children can do this alone but a younger child will need help.

GO
Make a paper strip loop by joining ends with glue or staples.
Add other strips, making interlocking loops.

FINGER PAINTING

Children love the "feel" of finger painting and of covering large open spaces with paint. Most of all they love the freedom to be messy without Mom and Dad getting angry!

Some children may be a little reluctant to "dive in," so try these hints for starting a hesitant beginner. Wet the child's hands with water before she starts, use a light colored paint mixed with liquid soap or use **warm** finger paint. All these tricks work to ease children into finger painting. For those who really don't like having dirty hands, rub on a hand cream before painting and put liquid soap or soap flakes in the paint. This makes removing the paint quick and easy.

Handprints

● HAVE READY
finger paint
flat dishes
paper
water and sponge
soapy water and towel
● GET SET
Put paint in flat dishes. With wet sponge, moisten table surface before placing paper on it, to keep paper from slipping.
● GO
Put a hand in paint, then place it firmly onto paper to make print. Make handprints in same or different colors, being sure to wash hands with soapy water between color changes.

Other things to try

- ***Print hands onto fabric to make a wall hanging.***
- ***Set paint dishes on the ground and make foot prints.***
- ***Cut out paper hands and feet, attach them to yarn and hang them as mobiles.***

What you need

Finger paint Finger paint can be bought at art supply or toy stores or you can make your own, following our simple recipes, opposite. Homemade paints can be colored with vegetable dyes, food coloring or powdered paint. To make homemade paint, begin by making your own paste or starch.

Paper If the finger painting is to be done on paper, choose large firm sheets. Construction paper and poster board are good for this purpose. The paper does not have to be white. Remember, the paper must be strong enough to stand up to squeezing and squelching. Moistening the table top with a damp sponge, before laying the paper on it, will hold the paper in place.

Covers and protectors Finger painting is messy so use a disposable or wipeable covering for the floor. The ideal covering for the floor is newspaper, which can be thrown away when you're done. If you have the space, encourage your child to work outdoors — it eliminates most clean-up problems. Painting smocks or old clothes, with sleeves which can be rolled up, are essential.

A low table Any flat surface will do. The best surface is one that can be easily cleaned or covered with plastic or waterproof material.

A bucket of soapy water, sponge and towel Place these near the work area for children to use *immediately* after they've finished painting to clean the table before the paint dries.

Space Provide somewhere to hang or lay paintings flat to dry.

HINTS

Liquid soap added to the paint will make hand cleaning easier.

Pine disinfectant added to the paint helps to keep it for a few days, as does storing it in the refrigerator.

A small quantity of cold water poured on top of finger paint will prevent a "skin" from forming on the surface.

Cornstarch paint
(makes a small quantity)
- 1 heaping tablespoon cornstarch
- 3 tablespoons boiling water
- coloring - vegetable dye, food coloring or powdered paint

In a saucepan, mix cornstarch with a little cold water to make a smooth white paste.
Add the water drop by drop, stirring all the time.
Pour on boiling water, stirring rapidly, until mixture is thick, clear and smooth.
(If it doesn't thicken, heat it until it does.)
Add color.

Cornstarch paint
(makes a larger quantity)
- 1 part cornstarch
- 3 parts boiling water
- coloring - vegetable dye, food coloring or powdered paint

In a saucepan, mix cornstarch in a little cold water to make a smooth white paste.
Add boiling water, stirring constantly.
Return saucepan to heat and boil until mixture clears.
Add color.

Laundry starch paint
You may need to vary this recipe a little, depending on the brand of starch you use.
- 1 part dry laundry starch
- 2 parts boiling water
- coloring - vegetable dye, food coloring or powdered paint

Mix starch with a little water to make a paste.
Add boiling water, stirring constantly. (If it doesn't thicken, bring to boil on stove.)
Add coloring.

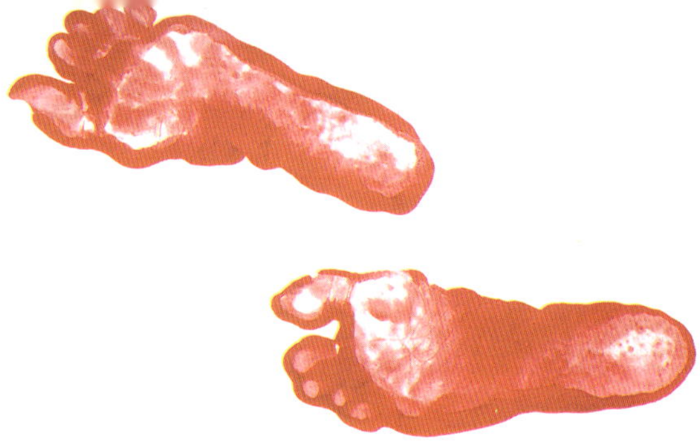

Footprints

- HAVE READY

large sheet of paper
tape or bricks
finger paint
flat wash tub or tray
bucket of soapy water
towel

- GET SET

This activity is best done outdoors. Tape paper to ground at both ends or secure it with bricks or some other suitable weights. Place paint in tub or tray at one end of paper.

- GO

Paint can be very slippery so it is important to hold child's hand as she makes the prints. Help child stand in paint and then walk the child along paper to make prints.
Keep bucket of soapy water nearby for washing feet.

Other things to try

- ***Make prints with washable soles of shoes.***
- ***Make footprints on the sidewalk, using water instead of paint.***

Foot painting can be done directly onto paper or on a waterproof surface. Spoon paint directly onto the surface. Sit the child on a low chair so he can use his feet to make pictures and patterns in the paint. When the painting is finished, place a fresh piece of paper over it, then carefully lift it off to make a print.

Finger painting

HAVE READY

- finger paint
- bowls or containers
- spoons
- strong paper
- water and sponge

GET SET

Spoon paint into bowls or containers.
Sponge table lightly with water and place paper on top. The damp surface will prevent paper from slipping.
Spoon paint from containers onto paper.

GO

Blend colors to make patterns and pictures using fingers and palms of hands. Hang painting to dry. Wash hands and painting surface.

Other things to try

- ***Let children paint directly on a table top covered with plastic. Then, with clean, dry hands they can lay a sheet of paper over the painting, gently patting or rubbing over the surface. Carefully lift off the paper to reveal the printed pattern.***
- ***Make patterns with spoon handles, forks, popsicle sticks, spools, sponges and cardboard combs, cut to make a variety of effects.***
- ***To change the texture of the paint, add salt, sawdust or rice to the paint. Or mix in some sand or dirt, instead of color, for "mud painting."***

DRAWING

At an early age, children enjoy the action of drawing and scribbling. Later, children may name and identify the scribbles they make, though you will not necessarily recognize them. Finally, symbols and patterns are developed and repeated — the cat your child draws actually starts to look like a cat!

The best way for a child to start drawing is with the paper firmly secured on the floor or table. Later, drawing can be done on a vertical surface, such as an easel, or on paper fixed to the wall.

Start with a sheet of paper, about 8 x 10 inches (25 cm x 20 cm), then as skills and concentration develop, provide larger sheets and introduce a variety of colors and textures in the paper.

Felt-tip pens are available in a great choice of colors and they're easy for young children to use. They can be used on most surfaces, including wax paper, plastic and fabric. Teach children to replace the cap on each pen after use.
Non-toxic, washable water-color pens are most appropriate for children. Permanent markers will stain clothing and bleed through paper.

Felt-tip pens

● HAVE READY
variety of non-toxic, felt-tip pens
paper
newspaper or cardboard

● GET SET
Place newspaper or cardboard underneath paper to prevent colors from bleeding through.

● GO
Let your child scribble away to his heart's content!

Other things to try

- ***Draw a tiny drawing on a balloon before blowing it up. Then blow up the balloon and watch the drawing grow!***
- ***Draw patterns around the edges of sheets of notepaper and around envelopes to match. Fold the notepaper in half to make a greeting card or stationery.***
- ***Draw a shape in one color. Draw around it again and again and again, changing colors each time.***
- ***Lay bottles and jars of different sizes on their sides and draw around the outside, then fill in the jar outlines with anything you like — jellybeans, ants, worms, monsters . . . !***

Chalk drawing

- HAVE READY

light chalk and dark paper
OR
colored chalk and light paper
cardboard
soapy water
sponge
towel

- GET SET

Use soapy water and sponge to clean hands during drawing.

- GO Color in light and dark tones.

Other things to try

- **Draw with chalk on wet paper for a very different effect.**
- **Mix one-third of a cup of sugar in a cup of hot water. When cool, wet chalk by dipping repeatedly into sugar solution while drawing.**

Above left: Chalk drawing on wet paper
Above: Drawing with wet chalk

Crayon drawing

Non-toxic, kindergarten-type chubby crayons are easiest for the youngest children to hold and control. Thinner crayons break more easily and are more tiring to use. Save them for older children.

- HAVE READY

colored, non-toxic crayons
paper
masking tape

- GET SET

Secure paper to table surface with tape.

- GO

Teach children to use the side of the crayon to cover large areas quickly and easily (see opposite page).

Crayon rubbing

● HAVE READY
non-toxic crayons
leaves
thin paper
cardboard and tape
● GET SET
Remove paper wrappers from crayons. Arrange leaves on cardboard or a flat surface. Tape paper in place over leaves.
● GO
Rub side of crayon lightly all over paper. Lift paper off to reveal shape and texture of leaves.

Other things to try

- **Place familiar objects, such as keys, coins and combs, under the paper.**
- **Rub over embossed wallpapers, paper doilies and corrugated cardboard or wriggly things, such as rubber bands, string and shoe laces.**
- **Take paper outside and make rubbings of concrete paths, brick walls, bark and other interesting surfaces.**

Jigsaws

You may need to help with the cutting out on this one. Two simple pieces may be enough for the youngest child. Increase the number of pieces and complexity of shapes for older children.

● HAVE READY
a completed drawing
paste or glue
broad brush
cardboard
non-toxic crayon or felt-tip pen
scissors
● GET SET
Brush paste or glue over back of drawing.
Glue drawing onto cardboard, smoothing out all wrinkles.
● GO
When glue dries, turn over drawing and outline jigsaw shapes with crayon. Cut out shapes and reassemble them.

PAPER CRAFTS

Paper is the most exciting and inexpensive craft material. It can be folded, glued, painted on, drawn on, cut up, and even sewn with ease. Children of all ages enjoy working with paper, scissors and glue.

Collect pieces of paper in a "treasure" box or drawer. Toss in anything that looks interesting. Children love shiny, sparkling things. Foil-coated papers and glittery wrappings make "prized" scraps.

Provide your child with a pair of scissors, suitable for her age and size. Cutting isn't easy, so she'll sometimes need your help. Teach your child how to open and close the scissors and how to hold and move the paper. Most of all, teach your child how to keep her fingers out of the way when she cuts.

Make sure the paper is not too thin (it will be hard to hold and scissors will slip), or too thick (small children will not be strong enough to cut through). Give your child plenty of practice cutting up magazines and newspapers. Later all the pieces can be stuck on cardboard or paper to make a picture!

What you need

Paper All kinds of paper are wonderful for craft work. Collect a variety including different colors and textures such as: glossy, tissue, gift wrap, wallpaper, shopping bags, magazines, butchers' paper, crepe paper, newspaper, paper plates, doilies, greeting cards, foil, cellophane.

Scissors Children start by tearing paper but soon move on to cutting. It is important that childrens' scissors **will** actually cut. Give them small safety scissors with rounded tips, and remember there are both right- and left-handed scissors available. A left-handed child will become frustrated if she is forced to use "rightie" scissors.

Paste There are many pastes and glues suitable for children. They should be non-toxic and easy to handle. It is easy to make your own paste and we have included two recipes on page 41 for you to try.

Choose the right strength of paste or glue to suit the paper. It is very disappointing for a child to have a special creation fall apart. For light paper items, commercial pastes or one of our homemade pastes are suitable. For heavier items use white glue, clear hobby or craft glues.

Paper collage

Old paintings, postcards, magazines, foil and greeting cards can provide a great variety of colors and textures for collages. Children can tear or cut their own pieces of paper or you can pre-cut various shapes, sizes and colors for them.

● HAVE READY
firm paper or cardboard
paste
brush
scissors
variety of papers
containers
damp cloth or sponge

● GET SET
Sort paper by colors, shapes, types and size and place in separate containers.
Place a large piece of paper or cardboard on table as collage base.
Choose pieces of paper and tear or cut as necessary.

● GO
Brush paste onto back of paper pieces.
Stick in position on base to make patterns or a picture.

Other things to try

■ ***Draw or paint over the collage or on the base before beginning the collage.***

Mosaics

Mosaics take time and patience so begin with a small one.

● HAVE READY
scraps of colored paper of any size
firm paper or cardboard
scissors
paste
brush

● GET SET
Tear paper into tiny pieces.

● GO
Apply paste to a small area of firm paper or cardboard backing and stick down scraps of paper to form pattern or picture.

Other things to try

■ ***Draw on backing sheet first then paste pieces of paper in place over drawing.***

Picture fun

● HAVE READY
old magazines
firm paper or cardboard
non-toxic crayons or felt-tip pens
scissors
paste
brush
● GET SET
Cut out parts of different people and animals from magazines.
● GO
Rearrange parts and paste them onto background to make new people. Draw in extra details if you wish.

Other things to try

- ***Young children can begin by exchanging heads on two bodies.***
- ***Later, children can cut out from magazines, divide them into heads, bodies and legs, and mix and match. Have children make up stories about these characters.***

Snowflakes

For very young children it is best to begin with thick paper, folded in half only. Increase number of folds with increasing age and skill level. Young children may prefer to tear the design rather than cut it.

● HAVE READY
squares of paper
scissors
● GET SET
Fold paper square in half and then in half again. Fold diagonally to form triangle.
● GO
Cut out design all around edges.
Unfold paper to reveal snowflake.

Other things to try

- ***Older children can make more folds before cutting.***
- ***Different shaped papers can be used to make doilies.***
- ***Drawings and paintings can be used to make place mats and colorful decorations.***

Fold, dip and dye

● HAVE READY
paper toweling or napkins
food coloring or vegetable dye
water and containers — one for each color

● GET SET
Mix coloring or vegetable dye with water in shallow containers.

● GO
Fold paper in half and then half again.
Dip each corner of paper into a color, one at a time.
Unfold paper to reveal design. Allow to dry flat.

Other things to try

- ***Make more folds before dipping.***
- ***Cut out a snowflake (see page 35) from paper toweling and dye it.***

Paper weaving

To make the frame for the weaving, you'll need an old wooden frame, a hammer and 10 or 12 small nails OR a piece of sturdy corrugated cardboard and a craft knife. **We strongly suggest that an adult make the frame; let the children do only the weaving.**

● HAVE READY
strips of paper (also crepe paper, cellophane, ribbon, feathers, pipe cleaners, etc.)
frame (see instructions below) and string or yarn

● GET SET
To prepare frame, hammer nails, equally spaced, across top and bottom of old picture frame.
If using cardboard cut Vs into edges at top and bottom.
Children should use a small frame until they are comfortable with weaving.

● GO
Secure string or yarn at top left corner and wind it around nails, or through the Vs, from top to bottom, making parallel threads. Secure at end.
Weave paper in and out, across threads.

All-paper weaving

This activity is best for the child who already knows how to weave.

● HAVE READY
sturdy paper
strips of paper
scissors
paste, glue or staples

● GET SET
Fold sheet of sturdy paper in half. Starting from fold, cut slits across paper, stopping about 3/4 inch (2 cm) from edge. (Slits need not be straight or even.)

● GO
Weave paper strips in and out of slits.
Glue or staple each strip at both ends, before starting with next strip. This holds weaving in place.

COLLAGE

A collage is an arrangement of materials glued onto a flat surface, such as a piece of paper or cardboard. The wider the variety of objects and materials that are used, the more interesting the finished work will be. There is no limit to what can be used, so set aside a box to store interesting bits and pieces of fabric, string, paper, twigs and leaves. Choosing the raw materials for a collage is half the fun.

Your child can select a particular color scheme or type of material to be used. It is also interesting to work on a colored or oddly shaped background. The background may be part of the collage or it may be totally covered.

Let your child make a collage with a particular theme, such as "summer," "animals," "sleep" or "cars."

Some collages make wonderful wall decorations while others, such as the three-dimensional "city scene" in our chapter on Junk (page 55), can be a play area all by themselves.

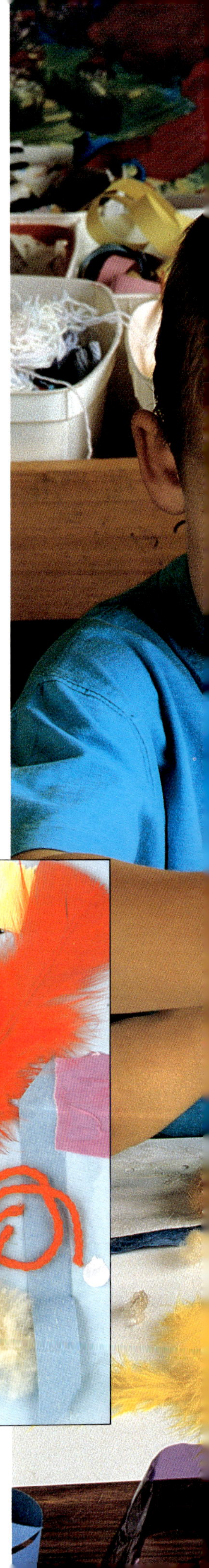

What you need

Materials A large variety of materials can be used for collages, but remember, too many choices may be confusing. Use this list of suggested materials as a starting point: bark, beads, bottle caps, small boxes, buttons, cardboard, confetti, cotton balls, dried beans, dried flowers, crushed egg shells, fabric, feathers, ferns, flowers, foil, grass, lace, leather, leaves, lids, muffin pan liners, net, nuts, pasta, paper, pebbles, ribbon, rope, sand, sawdust, seeds, shells, stamps, streamers, straw, string, toothpicks, twigs, woodshavings, yarn.

Staples and tape Masking tape is easiest for young children to use. If possible, put tape on a dispenser.

Crayons, felt-tip pens, colored pencils or paint are good for adding details. Make sure they're all non-toxic.

Scissors Provide a good pair of small scissors that cut easily.

Containers Put collage materials into various containers, so that it is easy to pick and choose from them. Any clean container will do.

Background material Use plain white paper, colored paper or even newspaper. Cut it into different shapes if you like.

Paste Paste and glue must be strong enough to hold the materials in place. For light pieces use homemade paste or school paste and for heavier ones try white glue, clear wood, hobby or craft glues. Glues can be applied in small squeeze bottles or by brush. You can also make your own paste using the simple recipes opposite.

CORNSTARCH PASTE

- $^1/_2$ cup cornstarch
- $^1/_2$ cup cold water
- boiling water

Mix cold water and cornstarch to make smooth white paste.
Quickly add boiling water while stirring. Stir until paste is clear.
If you plan to keep paste for several days, add a small amount of pine disinfectant and refrigerate.

ALL-PURPOSE FLOUR PASTE

- $^1/_2$ cup all-purpose flour
- $^3/_4$ cup cold water

Mix water and flour to make a smooth paste. Boil over low heat for several minutes, stirring continuously.
Thin with cold water, if necessary. If you plan to keep paste for several days, add a small amount of pine disinfectant and refrigerate.

Collage ideas

Collage requires gathering lots and lots of interesting objects and materials of different textures.
For a collage with a particular color or theme, keep an eye out wherever you go for collage "treasures."
A visit to the beach or the park can provide a wealth of raw materials, as can searching through the drawers and cupboards at home.

Theme collages are often the most fun. Collecting can become a wonderful activity all on its own and will test the ingenuity of the whole family. Base a collage on the beach, a farm, an airport or even a trip to the moon!

PUPPETS

Puppets are a wonderful way for children to express their ideas and creativity. One child can create a whole cast of characters to perform in the puppet shows he or she dreams up. From puppet people to monsters, animals or creatures of the imagination — puppets can be anything your child wants them to be. With a puppet, a shy child may even find the courage to "talk" to other people.

A puppet can be as simple as a face drawn on a finger and given a name and personality. An older child, with more skill and suitable materials, can make a very complex creation. The puppets on the following pages are intended only as sparks for the imagination. Don't reproduce them exactly. Much of the joy of puppet-making and play is in creating characters.

Teach your children how to make the puppet move. Quick, jumpy movement means the puppet is happy or excited. Slow, cautious movement may mean that the puppet is shy or frightened. Show them how to make the puppet dance, sing and, of course, take a bow. Before long, the kids will be entertaining you with their own, original puppet shows.

What you need

Scrap materials Old socks and gloves, cardboard tubes and boxes, sticks, pine cones, paper bags, paper plates, balloons, yarn, cotton balls, paper and cardboard are just a few things to save for making puppets.

Paste, glue, tape or staples hold the pieces together.

Scissors Provide a good pair of small scissors that cut easily.

Crayons, felt-tip pens and paint are good for drawing details. Make sure they're all non-toxic.

Space Provide an area that can be cleaned easily and a cloth or sponge for sticky fingers.

Finger puppets

● HAVE READY
felt or fabric
bits and pieces of yarn, ribbons, fabric, lace
glue and scissors
non-toxic felt-tip pens
needle and six-strand embroidery floss for older children

● GET SET
Fold felt or fabric in half. Draw a puppet shape, about 2 x 4 inches (5 x 10 cm), flat edge along bottom. Cut out through both thicknesses. Glue or stitch around edges. Leave bottom edge open. Glue or draw on a face and hair.

● GO
Insert fingers in bottom opening to bring the puppet to life.

Walking puppets

● HAVE READY
cardboard
completed drawing (optional)
non-toxic felt-tip pens
scissors
glue or paste
scraps of fabric, yarn, etc.

● GET SET
Draw a figure or paste a completed drawing onto cardboard.
Cut around figure and then cut out holes for "legs," large enough for a finger to poke through.
Decorate puppet by gluing on facial features, hair and clothes.

● GO
Put fingers through the holes and make puppet walk.

Paper plate puppet

● HAVE READY
paper plates
non-toxic felt-tip pens
collage materials (see page 40)
glue or strong paste
scissors
masking tape
sticks

● GET SET
Decorate a plate with pens and glued-on bits and pieces to make puppet's head. Tape a stick to back of plate for a handle.

● GO
Use stick handle to work puppet.

Finger family

● HAVE READY
non-toxic felt-tip pens (not permanent color!)

● GET SET
Draw friendly and ferocious faces on finger tips, so puppet fingers can bow and nod.

● GO
Find a shelf, banister or upturned box, and on with the show!

Paper bag puppet

● HAVE READY
small paper bags
non-toxic felt-tip pens or crayons
newspaper
stick or cardboard cylinder
tape or rubber band

● GET SET
Draw a face on a paper bag.
Fill bag with crumpled up newspaper.
Attach bag to stick or cardboard cylinder with elastic band or tape.

● GO
Use stick handle to work puppet.

Other things to try

- ***A small empty bag can go over child's hand without a handle.***
- ***Make puppet out of an old sock, decorated with a face and hair.***

Puppet on a stick

● HAVE READY
completed drawing or painting
scissors
cardboard (optional)
tape and paste or glue stick

● GET SET
Cut out puppet figure or head from the painting. You may have to paste it onto cardboard if paper is too light. Tape stick behind figure.

● GO Use stick to work puppet.

Other things to try

- ***Use a piece of decorated cardboard instead of a stick.***
- ***Make clothes out of paper or fabric for puppet and secure to stick with glue or tape.***

Finger people

HAVE READY
non-toxic felt-tip pens
fabric and paper scraps
scissors
masking tape

GET SET
Draw a face on one finger.
Wrap paper or fabric around finger for clothes and secure with masking tape.
Tear or cut out a circle of paper for a hat. Tear a small "X" in center of circle. Push finger into "X" to make hat.

GO
Move finger to bring puppet to life.

Rubber glove puppet

HAVE READY
rubber glove and non-toxic felt-tip pens and yarn or cotton balls

GET SET
Cut finger tips off rubber glove and draw faces on them with colored pens. Glue on yarn or cotton for hair or halo.

GO
Put glove finger tips on fingers.

KITCHEN PUPPETS

Familiar kitchen items can become terrific puppets in the wink of an eye. Try some of these great ideas to start you off.

Stella Strainer

● HAVE READY
strainer
paper
crayons or non-toxic felt-tip pens
scissors
glue or liquid starch
yarn and ribbon

● GET SET
Make eyes, mouth and nose out of paper and stick onto strainer with glue or starch. Thread yarn and ribbon through metal holes to make hair.

● GO
Perhaps Stella could sing a song or two?

Terrible Tongs

● HAVE READY
non-toxic felt-tip pens or crayons
tape, paper and egg carton
kitchen tongs
scissors

● GET SET
Tear cups from egg carton and draw on eyes. Tape eyes on tongs. Cut out a paper tongue and tape it on.

● GO
Animate the “terrible snapping tong monster” and don't forget the sound effects.

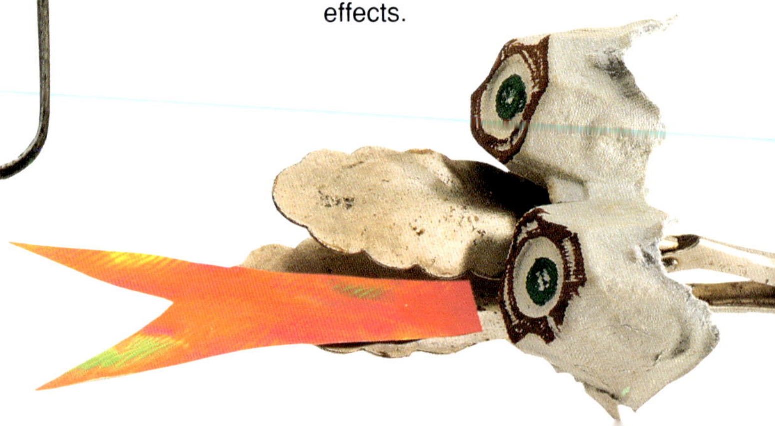

Sam Spoon

● HAVE READY
old wooden spoon or serving spoon
paper toweling or cloth; tape, rubber band or ribbon; non-toxic felt-tip pens

● GET SET
Arrange toweling or cloth around handle for clothes. Secure with tape, band or ribbon. Draw face on spoon.

● GO
Make two spoon puppets and they can act out a skit.

Other things to try

■ ***Use our "Fold, dip and dye" technique (page 36) to make clothes for Sam.***

Disby Dolly

● HAVE READY
dish scrubber
paper
scissors
paste or glue
dish cloth
rubber band
non-toxic felt-tip pens (not permanent color!)

● GET SET
Tear or cut out paper face and draw eyes and mouth onto paper. Tape face to scrubber. Place cloth around scrubber and gather at "neck." Hold dress in place with rubber band.

● GO Hold puppet by handle and make her dance

Other things to try

■ ***Cover scrubber with cloth or handkerchief and secure with rubber band. Draw puppet face on cloth.***

THEATRES & SHOWS

It's showtime! And a show needs a stage. Your home is probably full of potential "theatres" — a table turned on its side, a windowsill or the stair railing. With just a little effort you can make many simple stages for a puppet show. Cut the center out of an old sheet and hang it up on the clothesline or cut out a "screen" from the side of a large cardboard box and you have a TV set. For the very simplest puppet show, make a hole in the bottom of a paper cup and pop up your cast of characters.

Children like an audience for their puppets — someone to clap and cheer, ask questions or sing along. A "show" can last from ten seconds to ten minutes as children experiment and find out what "theatre" is all about.

Giant puppet

● HAVE READY
firm paper
stapler
crayons, paint or non-toxic felt-tip pens
newspaper
cardboard cylinder
tape
old clothes

● GET SET
Cut two sheets of paper the same size to make head.
Staple them together, leaving a hole at neck.
Paint or draw in face. Fill head with crumpled newspaper.
Tape head to a long cardboard cylinder.

● GO
These puppets are sure to give a "really big show"!

Other things to try

- ***Dress the puppet like a scarecrow with a second cardboard cylinder through the arms of a shirt and taped to the first cylinder at shoulder level.***
- ***Add streamers for hair.***

JUNK

Unwanted bits and pieces, that often get thrown away, are great raw materials for making things. You never know what will spark a child's imagination. Check our list of creative junk and remember — if it's safe and you have room, store it don't trash it!

What you need

Strong glue or tape for holding pieces together.

Scissors

Non-toxic paint, crayons and felt-tip pens for decorating

Bits and pieces for trimming, such as yarn, feathers and so on

Junk list — some ideas to start you saving				
balloons	cardboard cylinders	jewelry	paper plates	sticks and twigs
balls	cellophane	keys	pegs	stockings
bark	clothes hangers	lace	pine cones	string
bottle caps and tops	corks	leather	pipe cleaners	tinsel
bottles — plastic	cotton balls	lids	plastic containers	washers
boxes — all sizes	drinking straws	net	ribbons	wheels
buttons	egg cartons	paper	rope	wood scraps
cans	fasteners	paper bags	shells	yarn
cardboard cartons	foam meat trays	paper clips	spools	yogurt cups

JUNK BAND

Making music is fun. Making your own instruments is fantastic!

Strings to pluck

● HAVE READY
cardboard boxes, such as tissue or shoe boxes
big rubber bands in various widths
● GET SET
Cut a hole in the lid of a shoe box.
Stretch rubber bands around box, over the hole.
● GO Pluck bands, making a "tune" with different sized bands.

Other things to try

■ ***To make a guitar, cut a hole in one end of a stiff box. Fit a cardboard cylinder through the hole and tape it into place. Place rubber bands lengthwise around box. A stick squeezed under the bands at each end of the box will improve the sound.***

Bells

● HAVE READY
soft drink cans
yarn or string
tape and sticks
● GET SET
* Cut a length of string for each can. Break off a 1-inch (2.5 cm) piece from a stick. Securely tie one end of string to piece of stick. Feed tied stick through hole in top of can. Pull up so stick catches in can and tape securely in place. Repeat for other cans and tie strings together.
● GO Shake strings to make cans jingle.
*** This step should be done by an adult, or with an adult's supervision.**

Bottlephone

● HAVE READY
glass bottles
water and jug
vegetable coloring and eye dropper
metal spoon or stick
● GET SET
Using a jug, fill each bottle to a different level with water.
Put a drop of coloring in each bottle.
Place bottles in a row.
● GO
Strike bottles gently to hear different sounds. See how different levels of water affect the note. Play a tune and sing along.

Heavy metal music

● HAVE READY
clothesline
metal spoon or stick
string
metal objects such as kitchen utensils, metal tubing, bolts, large screws and so on

● GET SET
Tie metal objects onto clothesline so they hang freely.

● GO
Use metal spoon or stick to hit the objects.
See how different objects make very different sounds.

Other things to try

■ ***Put on a tape of a favorite song in the background and have the children play along.***

Drums

● HAVE READY
boxes, cans or plastic containers
sticks, dowels or wooden spoons
scissors or a hole punch
string or ribbon
● GET SET
Make two holes, opposite one another, on the sides near the top of drum.
Cut string or ribbon, long enough to go around the neck and thread through the holes.
Make knots in both ends of string, inside drum, so strap doesn't pull out.
● GO
Use sticks to beat drum.

Other things to try

- ***Make other drums which can be played while seated or carried on one arm and played with a stick or hand.***
- ***Make a whole drum kit for a rock band drummer.***

Maracas

● HAVE READY
paper plates
dried beans, pasta or rice
stapler
stick
tape
● GET SET
Cover a paper plate with an upside down plate of same size.
Staple around the edge, about three quarters of the way around.
Put beans inside plates and finish stapling around edge.
Tape a stick to the plates, or between the plates for a handle.
● GO
Shake, shake, shake!

Shakers

● HAVE READY
plastic bottles, small cans or plastic containers
things to rattle such as rice, sand, pebbles, seeds or pasta
strong glue and tape
paint or scraps of colored paper
● GET SET
Put a small number of rattle objects into an empty bottle or container.
Glue or tape lid securely in place.
This is important for very young children who might swallow small items.
Paint or decorate the outside of the shaker with paper.
● GO
Shake up the rhythm section of your very own band.

Other things to try

- ***Leave clear plastic shakers undecorated so contents can be "seen as well as heard."***
- ***Let children experiment making sounds using different amounts of filling in similar containers or same filling in different containers.***

Tooters

● HAVE READY
cardboard cylinder
wax paper
glue or paste and brush
rubber band
● GET SET
Put paste around outside of one end of cylinder. Cover end with a piece of wax paper. Hold paper in place with rubber band. Make a small hole in paper.
● GO Hum through the uncovered end of the cylinder, like a kazoo.

Other things to try

- ***Use a very long cylinder for a different sound.***

PRINTING

Printing is a little like magic! The shape of a familiar object is transferred onto another surface but in reverse.

The simplest kind of printing to begin with is "stamp-pad style." Before the child begins, demonstrate the steps for printing — a gentle dab on the paint pad, a look underneath to see if the shape is coated with paint and then a firm press onto the paper to make the print. Teach your child that it is important not to move the "stamp" sideways when pressing, in order to make a nice, clear print. Then carefully roll the stamp off the paper — don't lift straight up — for a good print.

Start with items that are easily held by small hands, such as pieces of wood, spools, plastic toys, bottle tops and cooking utensils. Pieces of sponge and fabric can be handled with a clothespin.

At first let children experiment with the action and make simple prints. Later as confidence grows they will be able to produce designs and pictures and try new ways of applying paint.

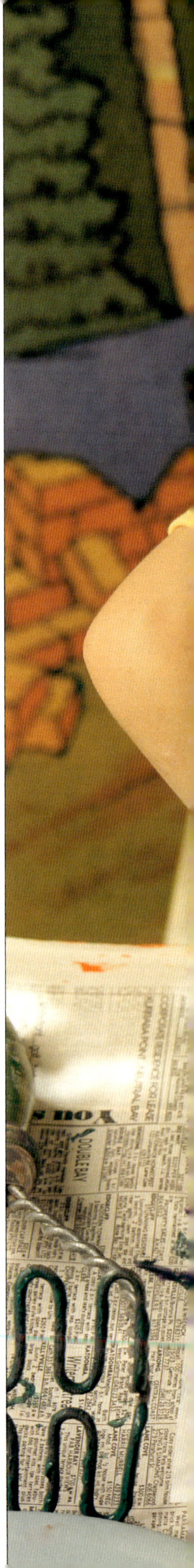

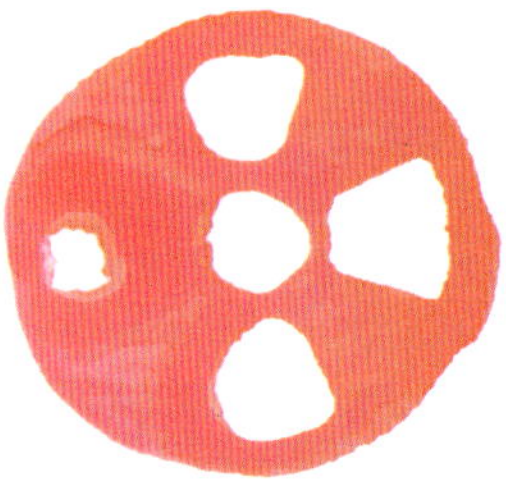

What you need

Shallow dish or tray Place a thin sponge or folded paper towel into the dish. Place the paint *under* the sponge or *on* the toweling and allow a few minutes for it to soak in.

Paints Those made with vegetable dyes or powdered paints are best. Be sure they are non-toxic.

Newspaper Place a pad of folded newspaper underneath the work to protect the table.

Thin sponge or paper toweling For paint pad.

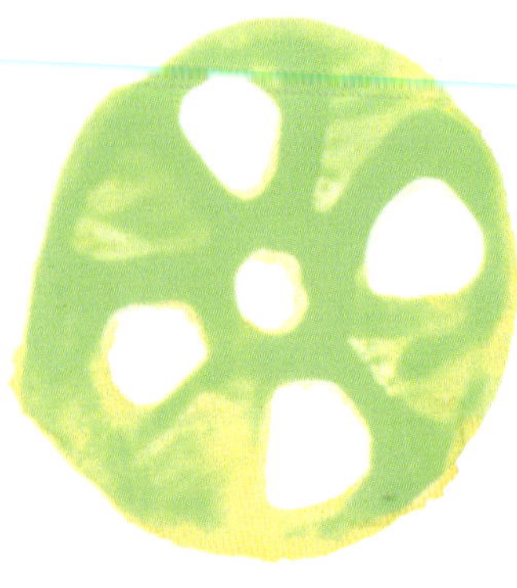

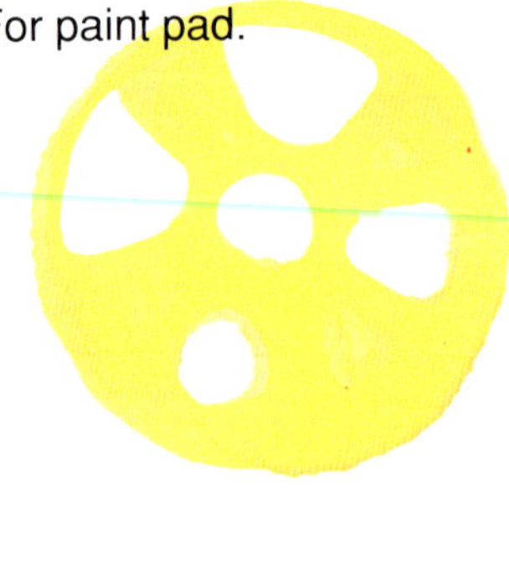

Fruit and vegetable printing

● HAVE READY

a variety of the following — potato, carrot, onion, cauliflower, pepper, orange, lemon, apple
paint pad, tray and paint
paper
paper toweling
knife

● GET SET

* Cut firm fruit or vegetables to create flat surfaces.
Place cut side down on paper toweling.
Press flat side of object down onto paint pad. Be sure it is well covered with paint.

● GO Press object firmly onto paper to make print.

*** This step should be done by an adult, or with an adult's supervision.**

Other things to try

- ***Cut potato into geometric shapes.***
- ***Older children can cut with a knife, or use a spoon, to make their own designs.***

Spattering

● HAVE READY

strainer or wire screen on a frame
tooth or nail brush
shallow dish
non-toxic thin paint or dye
paper
objects for printing, such as leaves, grasses, paper doily, paper shapes, kitchen utensils, etc.

● GET SET

Place objects on paper. Dip brush in paint and tap off any excess. Place strainer over objects. Protect the work area with newspaper and the "artist" with a smock.

● GO

Rub brush on wire, spattering paint on object and paper. Allow painting to dry flat. Remove objects to reveal printed shapes beneath.

Leaf and object printing

● HAVE READY

leaves or textured objects, such as corrugated cardboard, mesh, vegetable bags, lace, yarn, string
cardboard
paste or glue
scissors
tray
non-toxic thick paint and spoon
printing roller or paint roller
paper

● GET SET

Cut objects to size and arrange on cardboard. Glue in place and allow to dry.
Spoon paint into tray and work roller in it until it is covered with paint.
Roll paint onto objects so they are covered with paint.

● GO

Lay paper on top of cardboard and pat or rub over surface. Carefully remove paper to reveal print on the underside. Print can be repeated and more paint added in different colors.

Roller printing

● HAVE READY
non-toxic paint, pad and tray
paper
empty soft drink can,
cardboard cylinder,
rolling pin, plastic bottle,
hair roller, jar lid, spool,
etc.
cardboard
scissors

● GET SET
Roll different items on paint pad.

● GO
Roll on paper to make patterns.

Other things to try

- ***Glue string around roller to add an unusual texture. Allow the glue to dry before making print.***
- ***Glue pieces of cardboard onto roller to make unusual patterns in the print.***

MODELLING

Holding, feeling, squeezing, pounding, pulling, pushing, pinching and patting — are the greatest fun! With dough and clay, children have the opportunity to do all these things and at the same time develop dexterity in their fingers and hands.

Modelling or sculpting encourages the use of imagination, as children mold a fantasy world populated by their own creations. Dough can be reused, changed around or reworked completely. Creations can be temporary, or in the case of clay, be kept for a very long time.

Combine dough and clay models with other toys to create a whole world of fantasy or just make a pile of clay marbles for a playtime game.

Like a lot of children's activities, the end product of sculpting is not as important as the joy of doing it. The role of the adult should be to provide the dough and the space to work in. Allow your children to experiment and play the game of creation.

You will need

Dough Dough can be plain or colored. Children should experience both — some will prefer one and some the other. Children love to mix colors together, watching a rainbow dough develop. There is a variety of recipes for making dough. Children can make the simplest, uncooked type themselves, with a little help or supervision.
Covered table Sculpting with dough can get messy, so provide a surface that can be easily cleaned and some old clothes or aprons to wear.
Flour in a shaker Dough gets sticky to handle so keep a little all-purpose flour, to sprinkle over it while working.

Cooked dough

- 2 cups all-purpose flour
- 1 cup salt
- 2 tablespoons vegetable oil
- 4 tablespoons cream of tartar
- 2 cups water
- coloring (optional)

In a saucepan, mix dry ingredients. Gradually add oil and water, stirring them in together. Cook on top of the stove for 2-5 minutes, stirring constantly. The dough is cooked when mixture leaves side of pan and forms a mass. Cooked dough will keep for up to three months in a sealed container in the refrigerator.

Other things to try

- ***Add some simple equipment to use with dough, such as rolling pin, cookie cutters, blunt knitting needles, garlic press, plate for cutting around and so on.***
- ***Add texture to the dough by mixing in some rice, pasta or beans.***
- ***Add items to press into the dough to make patterns, such as a fork, spool, lids, lace, leaves and sticks.***

Uncooked dough

- 2 cups all-purpose flour
- 1 cup salt
- food coloring (optional)
- 2 tablespoons vegetable oil
- approximately 1 cup water
- bowl
- mixing spoon

Mix dry ingredients in bowl with spoon, add oil.
Add food coloring to water. Add water to bowl, a little at a time, stirring at first, then mixing with hands and kneading.
Dough can be kept in a floured container or plastic bag. If you are planning to keep it for a week or more, put it in the refrigerator in an airtight container.

Baker's clay decorations

Children can make this simple baker's clay with a little help and supervision. The quantities in the recipe must be used exactly as given. They cannot be halved or doubled.

● HAVE READY

4 cups all-purpose flour, unsifted
1 cup salt
1 1/2 cups water
bowl
utensils, such as a rolling pin, blunt knife, fork, toothpicks,
hair pins, wire or paper clips
non-toxic felt-tip pens, paint and brushes
clear gloss enamel or polyurethane

● GET SET

Mix salt and flour in bowl.
Add water, mixing with fingers. If clay is too stiff, add a little more water.
When mixed, take clay out of bowl and knead for about 4-5 minutes.

● GO

Roll and shape decorations and place on baking trays.
Insert hair pins, wire or paper clips into backs of decorations, to make hooks. Bake in moderate oven (about 325°F/160°C) at least one hour.
* Decorations can be colored with paint or pens and made more durable by painting with clear gloss enamel or polyurethane.

This is an alternative baker's clay that doesn't actually need baking.

● HAVE READY

2 cups baking soda
1 cup cornstarch
1 1/2 cups cold water

● GET SET

In a saucepan, mix baking soda and cornstarch.
Add water, mixing until smooth.
*Boil one minute, stirring frequently, until the texture is like mashed potatoes.
*Put on plate and cover with damp cloth until cool.
Knead and roll out dough.

● GO

Shape decorations and let them dry before decorating.

*** This step should be done by an adult, or done with an adult's supervision.**

Clay

You might be lucky enough to live in an area where you can find clay naturally in the earth. If you are not so fortunate you can buy modeling clay from art supply or craft stores. Children can work the clay with their fingers, like kneading, and slap and bang ("wedge") it on the table top to remove air bubbles. Keep working the clay in this way until the clay is soft. Roll the clay into balls and push a thumb into each ball. Fill the hole with water and cover with a damp cloth. This will keep the clay soft. If it does dry out, break it up and soak it in water for a day or two. When the clay is again soft, pour off the water and spread the clay out to dry a little. Clay will keep virtually indefinitely, especially in an airtight container.

Clay is messy, so provide a surface that can be wiped clean. Have a spatula or scraper and a bowl of water nearby for cleaning up and washing hands.

Children can use the same equipment for clay as for dough. Leave clay somewhere out of the way to dry out, but not in the sun. Paint it later if you wish or an adult can varnish it with clear enamel.

THREADING

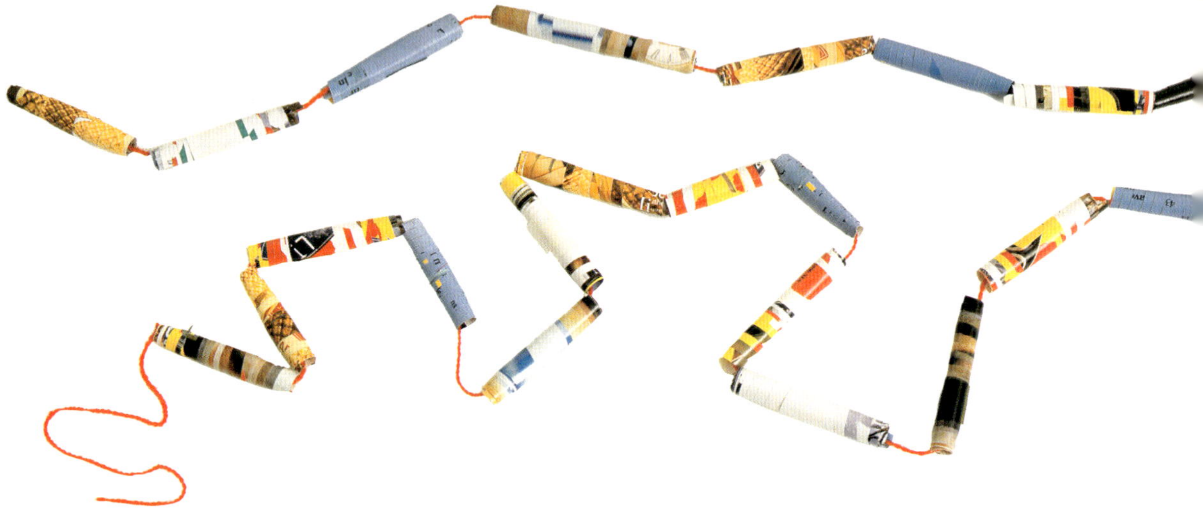

Children love to sort and arrange things. Threading fancy beads onto a cord or string will keep them busy for hours. It also helps to develop their dexterity and coordination.

In the beginning, use short beads with large holes that are easy to string. Use a fairly stiff cord, such as plastic tubing, coated electrical wire, shoelaces or waxed dental floss. Wrapping the end of a string with plastic tape also makes it easier to string beads.

A blunt needle, metal or plastic, can also be useful for stringing beads. After you've threaded the needle, knot both ends to prevent it from pulling out of the needle and to keep the beads on the string.

Paper beads

HAVE READY
old magazines
blunt or darning needle
yarn or string
scissors
glue

GET SET
Cut color pages of magazines lengthwise to make long triangles, about 2 inches (5 cm) wide at the base and 11 inches (30 cm) tall. Cut a length of cord for necklace, thread it through needle and knot behind eye so it won't pull through.

GO
Starting from wide end of triangle, roll paper around needle.
Put glue on pointed end of paper triangle and press down to complete bead.
Continue making beads on the needle and pushing them along the thread. When there are sufficient beads on the cord, tie the ends together securely.

WEAVING

Some kind of frame or loom is needed for weaving but it doesn't have to be an expensive one. A forked stick, cardboard box, foam meat tray, chicken wire or paper plate all may be used as frames. Make sure the weaving and frame are not too large for the child to manage and that they are positioned to be easy to work on. Cover sharp ends of the frame with tape.

Cut yarn, string, paper and fabric in lengths, ready for weaving. And if using a blunt or darning needle, tie the threads behind the eye, so they don't pull out.

Weaving in a tree

Two horizontal branches form the "frame" for this weaving. If you don't have a tree to use, a forked branch will yield a very similar effect.

● HAVE READY
long strips of fabric, yarn or string
long grasses and reeds
feathers
strips of colored paper

● GET SET
Find a suitable branch for the top and a smaller one for the bottom. Tie lengths of fabric, yarn and string between the upper and lower branches.

● GO
Weave in and out across these "strings" using some of the materials we suggest and any others you can find around the house or garden

Other things to try

■ **Once the basic weaving is complete, add dried flowers and leaves, twigs and interesting seed pods.**

God's eye

HAVE READY
two long sticks or twigs
yarn or string

GET SET
Cut lengths of yarn.
Cross two sticks and tie together securely where they cross.

GO
Holding sticks in an "X", weave yarn under and over sticks, working from center to outside. Tie ends of yarn together to change colors.

Other things to try

Older children can weave the yarn over one stick, then around and under the stick, then move yarn to next stick, continuing from center to outside, and tying yarns to the sticks when changing colors. They may also be able to handle the yarn in small balls instead of cut lengths.

Weaving on a tray

● HAVE READY
foam meat tray
craft knife
scissors
darning needle
yarn, ribbon, strips of paper,
feathers and so on

● GET SET
*With a knife, cut a window in tray.
*Thread needle and tie knot.
Push needle through tray. Turn tray over and pull thread through. On opposite side of window, make a similar hole and pull thread through. Continue making parallel "strings" across the window. When finished tie knot in yarn and cut off any excess.

● GO
Weave lengths of yarn, paper or ribbon across the strings. There is no need for regular "under-over" weaving, an irregular texture is very attractive.

*** This step should be done by an adult, or done with an adult's supervision.**

SEWING

Sewing is just another way of "painting" a picture or making a design, using threads instead of paints. For very young children, sewing for the first time, it is best to use firm open-weave fabric, such as burlap, or even plastic needlepoint canvas. You can draw the design onto the fabric first, if you prefer, or just "draw" the picture with needle and thread.

● HAVE READY
yarn in assorted colors
burlap, fabric or plastic needlepoint canvas
large-eyed, blunt needle, metal or plastic scissors
● GET SET
Cut lengths of yarn, about 18 inches (45 cm) long.
*Thread needle and tie yarn behind eye so it won't pull through.
Knot end of yarn.
● GO
Sew freely over fabric, pushing needle through and pulling up thread each time, before making next stitch.
*** This step should be done by an adult, or done with an adult's supervision.**

Other things to try

■ ***Draw a picture on fabric with magic markers and follow line with stitches.***
■ ***Make "sewing cards": With a hole puncher, make holes in a piece of shirt cardboard and sew around holes.***
■ ***Or, draw a picture on a piece of shirt cardboard. Cut out drawing and make holes around the edge. Sew through the holes.***

The Rainy-Day Box

Collect and save these everyday items and leftovers for rainy-day crafting.

Paper — newspaper, gift wrap, wallpaper, cardboard, colored paper and foil.

Fabric — scraps of materials in different textures, colors and weights.

Cardboard tubes, cylinders and boxes

Yarn — different weights, colors and textures.

Old kitchen utensils — particularly strainers and wooden spoons, which make wonderful puppets, drumsticks and musical instruments.

Bottle caps and corks

Ribbons, cords and string

Discarded costume jewelry

Shells

Bark, pine cones and interesting seeds

Buttons

Wood — short twigs and smoothly sanded workshop scraps.